Who Ya Gonna Call?

The Kid's Directory for Self Help
[There's always someone to help!]

written by: Carole Marsh Longmeyer
illustrated by: Susan Van Denhende

Illustrations and design by Susan Van Denhende

Editing by Janice Baker

Art Director John Hanson

WHILE WE HAVE PROVIDED SOME NUMBERS, YOU WILL NEED TO REFER TO YOUR PHONE BOOK OR THE INTERNET TO GET SOME OF THE LOCAL NUMBERS THAT WOULD BE BEST FOR YOU TO HAVE!

Bluffton Books
blufftonbooksandmore.com

GALLOPADE

Who Ya Gonna Call?

Guess what? It will not be Ghostbusters! Do you ever worry or wonder who's going to dash to your side...run to your aid... rescue your cute little body in case of an Emergency...or just a Big Problem?

Guess what? YOU are going to help yourself! How? By grabbing this easy to use A-to-Z directory of people or places to call. Yes, it is fun and funny to read and look at, but this book is also Serious Business. So keep it with your phone, or stash it in your book bag. You just never know when you might really need it (so do not hide it under your mattress or toss it in the dirty clothes basket).

YOU can be the hero, even if the person who needs help...is YOU!

4 COULD YOU DELIVER A BABY?

It does not happen often, but some kids have had to deliver their new brother or sister. Like the Boy and Girl Scouts–be prepared! If you find yourself having to help deliver a baby, here are some tips!

Stay calm; babies are born all the time! Call 9-1-1! Try to answer any questions they ask you; you may have to ask the mother.

Listen to the 9-1-1 instructions; they will stay on the line and help you. (Put your phone on "speaker" so you can hear, but keep your hands free.)

Remember: The mother is going to have the baby; you are just helping out.

Talk nicely to the mother and ask what you can do to help. Putting towels under or over her may help. Ask her to lay still and not get up and leave; tell her that help is on the way.

Do not be afraid if the mother is in pain or cries out; labor pains do hurt but they are natural.

Be patient. The baby may not come as quickly as you think; that is ok.

If the baby is born, it will be slippery, so try to catch it with a towel or some other cloth. Do not drop the baby! If the "cord" is attached to the baby's belly button, don't worry; just leave it there. Try to wrap the baby in a cloth or blanket and keep it warm until help comes.

Who Ya Gonna Call?

Nine long months ago my mom said, "I am going to have a baby!"
So, now it looks like she really is.

Uh, oh, I mean NOW!
Oops, like maybe RIGHT NOW!

Who ya gonna call?

The AMBULANCE!: 911

5 AMBULANCE

6 BITE AND STING TIPS!

Most insect bites or stings are harmless. If you have been stung or bitten, you might feel:

pain
swelling
a stinger stuck in your skin

What to do:

Remove any visible stinger with tweezers; you can also scrape the stinger off with a credit card or a clean fingernail.

Wash the bite or sting site with soap and water. Cover the site and keep it clean.

You can use a washcloth filled with ice to reduce pain and swelling.

If the person has trouble breathing, call 911 immediately!

Who Ya Gonna Call?

That dog is acting funny... What is that foam around its mouth? Did it get into the whipped cream?

Uh-oh, I think it might be rabies...

Who ya gonna call?

ANIMAL CONTROL!: ______________

TONGUE TIED!

Useful tips to keep your tongue in tip top shape!

Never stick your wet tongue (not even on a dare or as a joke) on something icy or wet and cold. It may look funny to have your tongue touch something like a cold pole, but it could get stuck and hurt.

If you bite your tongue or cheek or lip, you can run cold water over it to help stop the pain and any bleeding. If this does not help, get medical help or find an adult right away.

NEVER RUN WITH A SHARP OBJECT IN YOUR MOUTH!

Always take anything- popsicle stick, lollipop, candy cane, etc- out of your mouth before running, just in case you trip and fall.

Who Ya Gonna Call?

I found a stray dog...
No tag.
Mom says I cannot keep him.

He might belong to someone.

Who ya gonna call?

The ANIMAL SHELTER!:

AED TIPS!

If you look around, you might spot a square red or white box marked AED. (AED=Automatic External Defibrillator.) You can find them at pools, in public places like airports, libraries, or in many other places.

Now, an adult usually uses these things, but a kid could, too, in an emergency, like if someone was having a heart attack.

If you zip open the AED, you will see buttons you can push to start it. The machine will then "talk to you" and tell you what to do and when.

If you ever have to use one, just take your time, listen, and If you ever had to push the SHOCK button, be sure to stand clear and not touch the person.

Even if you find the AED, get it open, and so are ready to use the life-saving machine, an adult may show up and take-over, but you will have given them a head start!

Note: An AED will not shock a person unless they need it.

Who Ya Gonna Call?

It just figures- zombies have attacked!
Just what I need with summer vacation coming- some awful zombie disease.

I wonder if they are contagious?

Who ya gonna call?

The CENTERS FOR DISEASE CONTROL! : 1-800-232-4636

CDC

SWIMMING TIPS!

Never be shy when someone is in trouble in the water. If there are lifeguards around, they probably have seen the problem, but you never know!

If you see someone "drowning" do not wait to see if they are just kidding- call out for help LOUDLY!

Do not try to go in the water to help them yourself. Call out for an adult or the lifeguard to help them.

If for some reason you and a friend get a person out of the water and they are not breathing, try to put them face down. Call 9-1-1 and call out loudly for an adult or the lifeguard.

Who Ya Gonna Call?

The boat went out.
The boat did not come back...
We went out on the boat.
The boat went aground...

We do not want anyone to drown!

Who ya gonna call?

The COAST GUARD!: 911

THINGS TO AVOID!:

A pound of prevention may not be exactly equal to a pound of cure, but it sure helps. Avoid...

Allergic reactions: Wear an "I am allergic to __________" bracelet and know what you are allergic to.

Foot injuries: Do not wear flip-flops.

Poisoning: Keep anything toxic locked up! That includes the kitchen, bathrooms, and garage.

Choking: Take small bites, chew well!

Colds/Flu: Eat healthy, get enough sleep, exercise, and wash your hands often.

Sunburn: Wear sun block of SPF 30 or higher; apply often, especially after you get out of the water.

NEVER: Play with matches! Pick up a gun that you find! Ride without a seatbelt on! Smoke! Drink alcohol! Do drugs!

Who Ya Gonna Call?

You just never know when:

a. aliens might attack

b. a war will start

c. other

WHEN YOU NEED THE BIG GUNS...

Who ya gonna call?

The DEPARTMENT OF DEFENSE! : 703-697-5131

LIGHTNING SMART TIPS!

Pay attention to the weather and your surroundings; lightning is common in many places during the summer. Here are some tips to stay safe in a lightning storm:

Stay inside if you hear any thunder! If you get caught out in a thunderstorm, try to get inside. The stronger the building the better!

A house is better than a car. If you must get in a car, roll up the windows and keep your hands and feet off any metal.

Stay away from water, plumbing, and electrical equipment, even if inside during an electrical storm. Stay away from windows too.

Do not use a phone with a cord.

If caught outside, get away from a wide-open space or a high hill. Do not get under a tree! Try to get inside.

Who Ya Gonna Call?

It is Halloween. It is dark and spooky. There are vampires at the front door.
The candles go out.
You turn on the lights...

The power is out!

Who ya gonna call?

The ELECTRIC COMPANY!

OOPS- WHAT IF...

...something bad happens, like a body part gets cut off? While we do not want to think of accidents such as this (too gross!), keep your cool and do these things:

Call 911.

Find an adult to help you right away, especially to help stop the bleeding.

If a body part is just partially torn off (say from a dog bite or accident), try to help hold the part so it will stay attached with a clean towel or other cloth.

If the body part, a finger, for example, is completely severed, try to find it. Wrap the finger in gauze or a clean washcloth and put it in a plastic sandwich bag and seal it up.

Put this bag in another plastic bag, a larger one, filled with some ice and water. You could also put it in an ice cooler. Do not freeze the body part!

Be sure the body part goes to the hospital with the patient! Doctors may be able to reattach it.

Who Ya Gonna Call?

I got in the elevator in
Grandma's condo.
The elevator started...
The elevator stopped!
I was stuck between floors!

Instead of panicking, I thought...

Who ya gonna call?

The ELEVATOR EMERGENCY!: 911 (call from the elevator phone)

BIKE SAFETY TIPS!

ALWAYS WEAR A HELMET! Looking cool will not seem that important if you ever get into an accident.

Try not to ride on roads that have traffic or that have no "shoulder" (a place on the side where you can pull off). Maintain your bike so that a flat tire, loose chain, etc. will not cause you to lose control or crash.

If you ride at night, always wear as much reflective clothing as possible. Have a headlight, taillight, and stick reflective tape on your shirt front and back, on your bike, and on the backs of your pedals.

Bike safely. Always follow road signs like a STOP sign. Always look left and right, then look again before crossing a road. Try to ride with a "bike buddy" so you can look out for each other.

Try not to bike barefoot or in flip-flops; wear enclosed shoes like sneakers when you can.

Who Ya Gonna Call?

The hurricane came!
The hurricane went!
So did our house!
The trees! My bike!
My book bag!

My homework (oh, well).

Who ya gonna call?

The Federal Emergency Management Agency!: 1-800-621-3362

BURN TIPS!

Avoid sunburns; they are serious! Use sun block before and after you get in the water; use frequently and use enough of it! If sunburned skin hurts, you can use a spray made for sunburns.

For other kinds of burns:

Call 911 right away if it is a bad burn, covers a lot of area, if the person has trouble breathing, or is very young or very old. In the meantime, keep the person still and calm.

Do not put ice or ice water on a burn. Do not remove clothing stuck to a burn. Do not touch a burn or try to clean it. Do not break blisters. Do not use ointment on a burn.

If a burn is minor, you can run cold water over it to reduce pain. Seek help for any burn right away.

Who Ya Gonna Call?

STOP!

DROP!!

ROLL!!!

SMOKEY THE BEAR, WHERE ARE YOU WHEN I NEED YOU?

WHO YA GONNA CALL?

The FIRE DEPARTMENT!: 911

FIRST AID TIPS!

Here are some things you can do to be prepared for some common emergencies!

Build a First Aid kit!

Learn the Heimlich Maneuver to help someone who is choking!

Make a list of neighbors, doctors, and others you might need to call on in the middle of the night!

Learn CPR! (Cardio Pulmonary Resuscitation)

Make a list of local Urgent Care places and their hours (all are not open 24 hours or weekends), and their addresses and phone numbers.

Build Your Own First Aid Kit!

Find something to hold it all: a back pack, small ice cooler, a plastic box, a beach or tote bag- whatever works!

Things to put inside (any or all will help!): band-aids in various sizes, a thermometer, adhesive tapes, antiseptic wipes, antibiotic ointment or spray, a pair of scissors, a roll of bandages or a pack of gauze pads, tweezers, a First Aid booklet, disposable gloves

Who Ya Gonna Call?

Oh, dear!
Smokey the Bear is not gonna be happy! Someone has left their campfire smoldering!

That could easily start a forest fire!

Who ya gonna call?

The FIRE DEPARTMENT!: 911

YOU ASKED ABOUT ASTHMA...

What if you encounter someone who is having an asthma attack (difficulty breathing)?

Stay calm; this will help them stay calm. Help them to sit down and get comfortable.

If they have anything tight around their neck or stomach, such as a book bag strap or a belt, help them loosen it so they can breathe better.

Ask if they have their "medicine" or "inhaler." They may indicate a purse or book bag; find it and give it to them...they will know how to use it.

If nothing seems to help them breathe better very soon, call 9-1-1. If people are nearby, call out for an adult to come and help you.

Who Ya Gonna Call?

You smell gas!
(It is not your brother's fault this time.)

So after going outside...

Who ya gonna call?

The GAS COMPANY!: ____________________

28 ALLERGIC REACTION TIPS!

As you probably know, many people—even kids—can be very allergic to certain things: for example, a bee sting, food (like peanuts), or something else. If you encounter someone having a bad allergic reaction, it might look like:

a. they cannot breathe very well
b. they act weak, dizzy, confused, or scared
c. they have a sudden rash or big bumps over their face or neck
d. more than one of the above

What to do:

Ask if you can help. If they cannot talk, they may nod or wave "yes" to you.

Ask if they have their "medicine;" this may be a kind of "pen" they stick themselves with. If they indicate their purse or book bag, etc., find it as quickly as you can and give it to them.

If they are unable to "stick" themselves with their "pen," help them if they can indicate what you should do.

If the person is getting worse or passes out, call 9-1-1 and call out for any nearby adult to help you.

Who Ya Gonna Call?

Gee, whiz...my teacher said I had to have all of my "immunizations" before I could come to school. What are they? Where do I get them?

Do they, uh, involve NEEDLES?

Who ya gonna call?

The HEALTH DEPARTMENT!: ____________________

WHAT IF...

If you find yourself around an older adult who suddenly acts confused, sick, or has fainted or fallen:

If they are conscious (awake):

Ask them if they are ok, then if they need anything, such as their glasses, hearing aids, or a glass of water.
If they still feel unwell or are hurt, find an adult or call 9-1-1. Stay with them; try to keep them calm and sitting or laying down.

If they are unconscious (have fainted or passed out):

Let them sit or lay where you found them.
Call 9-1-1.
Call out for someone to help you.
You can cover them with a blanket.
Wait until help arrives.

If they have fallen:
Do not try to move them.
Call 9-1-1. Call out for someone to help you.
Cover them with a blanket and wait until help arrives.

Who Ya Gonna Call?

Maybe you need the name of a doctor?
Or to see what room your friend is in?
Or if the gift shop can deliver flowers to a new Mom?

Or a lot of other things!

Who ya gonna call?

The HOSPITAL!: ______________________

NOSEBLEED TIPS!

If someone gets a nosebleed, here are some things you can do:

Sit with your head slightly forward; pinch the nostrils together for about 10 minutes.

If this does not stop the bleeding, put pressure on the upper lip just below the nose.

You can also put an ice pack on the bridge of the nose, but do not apply ice directly to the skin. Put a clean washcloth or some other dressing between the ice and the skin.

If the bleeding does not stop, get medical help or find an adult to help.

Who Ya Gonna Call?

Uh, no, I do not have any Reeses Pieces.

Uh, no, I do not speak Schlamagon.

Uh, no, I do not have any jumper cables.

Uh, no, I do not have the number for a Holiday Inn...

Who ya gonna call?

NASA!: 1-202-358-0001

BOY, IT'S HOT/COLD!

Good Tips for Summer!

Stay hydrated! Drink lots of water. Gatorade is good too.

If you have stomach cramps, nausea (feel like you will throw up), or other symptoms of heat exhaustion: Move to a cooler place. Lightly stretch tight muscles. Only start activity again slowly; rest is best!

If you get worse, get medical help as soon as you can.

Good Tips for Winter!

Dress in layers to stay warmer.

Wear socks and mittens to avoid frostbite when it is really cold; better to be warm than "look cool"!

Drink lots of water in winter, too!

Shivering or teeth-chattering is a sign your body wants to get warm; get inside!

Who Ya Gonna Call?

You spy a tornado funnel... You see hail as big as tennis balls!

You see snow in July?!?

Who ya gonna call?

The NATIONAL OCEANIC AND ATMOSPHERIC AGENCY! : 1-877-633-6772

36 HOW TO HELP LOST KIDS!

Kids get lost sometimes- it is true! If you find a lost kid, here are some things you can do to help.

If a little kid is lost, stay with him or her; stay put and see if the parent finds you, instead of wandering off to look for the parent.

Keep the little kid calm: smile and talk gently. If they do not want you to hold them, stoop down in front of them or sit beside them.

Ask the little kid questions: What is your name? How old are you? This will help keep them calm until adult help comes.

If you are going to do anything to a child you do not know, show them first, such as pretending to put a band-aid on their doll or teddy bear.

Who Ya Gonna Call?

He is turning RED!
His head is getting BIGGER and BIGGER!
"YIIIIIIIIIIIIIIIIIIIIIIIIIIIIII!"

He is stuck! This is going to take a pro!

Who ya gonna call?

The PARAMEDICS!

911

POISONOUS PLANT TIPS!

Try to stay away from plants like poison ivy, poison sumac, and poison oak! However, if you find yourself scratching a sudden red rash, you can try the following!

Take off any clothing, like a shirt or socks, that have been exposed to the plant.

Wash the area of the skin that itches with soap and water as soon as you can.

Use a paste of baking soda and water, or Calamine lotion, on the rash.

Do not scratch!

See a doctor if it gets worse.

Who Ya Gonna Call?

You are babysitting your pesky younger sister.
Why is her head so hot? Why is she barfing all over your new shirt? Why is that bottle of yucky stuff under the sink on the counter?

Who ya gonna call?

POISON CONTROL! 1-800-222-1222

WHAT TO DO IF...

You know to call the police if you ever get robbed, but what is best to do when you first walk in the house and discover the robbery?

If you go into the house and notice things are missing or have been moved, get out! Do not go through more of the rooms to check what is missing- you can do that later. It is safer to leave, just in case the robber is still there.

Do not touch anything! Whether it is your stuff that has been moved, something the robber left behind, or even the lightswitch, it is important evidence. Touching something could cover up the robber's fingerprints.

Things you can do to help prevent a robbery:

Install a security system.

Install a 2nd deadbolt- the higher the better!

Do not open the door for anyone you do not know if your parents are not home.

If you leave for vacation, call the post office to stop the mail.

Have a friend pick up your newspaper so they do not pile up in the driveway. They can also keep an eye on the house.

Who Ya Gonna Call?

Someone has stolen everything in the yard!
Your bike...Mom's favorite ugly fountain...all the shrubbery...the garage! The dog! Even the trash can!

No, it is not an emergency, but...

Who ya gonna call?

The POLICE!: 911

TOOTH TIPS!

If someone gets a tooth knocked out:

Help control the bleeding by placing a rolled piece of sterile dressing over the hole. If the person is ok, you can have them rinse their mouth with cold water, then apply the dressing.

Find the tooth! Save the tooth! Pick the tooth up only by the enamel part (not the root part). Put the tooth in a paper cup of milk, or if no milk is available, cool water.

Get the person and the tooth to a dentist as soon as possible. It is possible the tooth can be put back in and saved.

Who Ya Gonna Call?

Ooooh, I have a tummy ache!
I think I ate too much...
vaaayyyyy too much!

I really vant to donate some blood!

Who ya gonna call?

The RED CROSS! : 1-800-733-2767

COMPUTER SAFETY TIPS!

Never give out personal information on the computer (name, age, address, telephone number), and never send a picture of yourself over the computer without your parent's permission.

Tell your parents right away if anyone or anything you read on the computer makes you uncomfortable.

Do not forget that people can lie on the computer–someone can use a different name or be an adult, not a kid.

Never write to someone you do not know. Never meet someone you met over the computer, or let them visit you, without your parent's permission.

Who Ya Gonna Call?

I was bullied at school today! Imagine that! I know I need to report it to someone, but who?

I got out my local telephone book and found these ideas!

Who ya gonna call?

The COUNSELOR! : ______________________

The PRINCIPAL! : ______________________

BOO-BOO TIPS!

Some "boo-boos" just need a simple band-aid, maybe with some antiseptic on beforehand. But if someone gets a worse wound, here are some tips:

For a smaller wound such as a skinned knee where skin is broken and there is bleeding: Use a clean cloth and press on the wound a few minutes to stop bleeding. Wash the wound with soap and water. Apply antibiotic ointment. Cover with a bandage or oversized band-aid.

For a more serious wound, try to get an adult to help right away. Until then: Cover the wound with a clean cloth and press firmly to help stop bleeding. Cover the wound with a tight bandage; if blood comes through, add another bandage. Keep the person calm and still.

Wash your hands before and after helping someone with a wound that is bloody, if you can.

Who Ya Gonna Call?

Oops, my horse kicked my dog...
My dog bit my cat...
My cat scratched my gerbil...
My gerbil ate my goldfish...
And my rabbit fell out of a hat!

Who ya gonna call?

The VETERINARIAN!: ______________________

MORE SWIMMING TIPS!

Swimming is fun. Learn to swim! If possible, take Red Cross swimming and water safety classes. Even if you can swim, never swim alone, and follow these other swim safety smart tips!

If you cannot swim, be careful around the water– do not accidentally fall in. If you are going in the water, wear a good flotation device.

Be sure your friends know that you are not yet a swimmer. Stay in the shallow part of the pool. In a lake, always assume any part is over your head.

Swim where there is a lifeguard, if at all possible. Have a swim "buddy" so you can look out for one another. Never hesitate to call for help if you cannot find your swim buddy or one of you gets in trouble in the water.

Who Ya Gonna Call?

Something happened while I was at school and mom and dad were at work—our house has turned into a FISH TANK!

Where is the water cut-off? Where is my diving bell? Who has a submarine I can borrow?

Who ya gonna call?

The WATER DEPARTMENT!: ______________________

GREAT SAFETY TIPS!

Stay cool and calm in an emergency!

Know how to call 9-1-1.

Stay with a hurt person (or your family, car, etc.) until help arrives.

Never stay in a house where you smell "gas." Get out and call 9-1-1 immediately.

Always look both ways before you cross a street; then look again!

Use crosswalks; don't "jaywalk"!

Always wear your seatbelt!

Never leave the stove on while you are out of the room. Check and be sure it is off before you leave the house.

Always keep poisonous substances locked up.

Wear safety goggles when tools recommend it.

Who Ya Gonna Call?

I have this assignment that requires me to go "right to the top" to answer some questions about American history.

Who were the founding fathers? Did George Washington really cut down that cherry tree?

Who ya gonna call?

The WHITE HOUSE! : 202-456-1414

INDEX

INDEX

INDEX

INDEX

ABOUT THE CREATORS

Hi, I'm Carole Marsh!

I wrote this book because I sure could have used it when I was a kid. I can use it now! You just never know when something will happen, and I want to be prepared to save the day! Maybe I have a Super Hero complex, or maybe I'm just a big chicken livered scaredy cat? Either way, keep your book handy...and hope you never have to use it except to swat flies!

Little is known about Susan Van Denhende, except that the last "e" in her last name is silent. Besides having a hard to pronounce last name, it is known that she recently graduated from SCAD and wants to illustrate books and comics for kids. It is rumored that she had a phobia of phones as a child, which is ironic as almost every non-art job she's had has involved answering phones. Though she refuses to answer her phone when called, her voicemail indicates that she is thrilled to be drawing phones instead of answering them.